You Know What Old People Are Like

Written by Jack Gabolinscy
Illustrated by Paul Könye

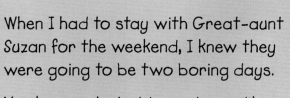

When I had to stay with Great-aunt Suzan for the weekend, I knew they were going to be two boring days.

You know what old people are like. They water the pot plants in the morning, watch TV all afternoon and feed the cat at night. Then they have to go to bed early because they've had such a busy day.

3

Mum left me at Aunt Suzan's gate.
"Have a nice holiday," she called as she drove off.

It didn't feel as if I was going on holiday. It felt as
if I was going to prison to be locked away from
the world for two days.

Aunt Suzan met me at the front door.

"Quick, Ellie!" she said. "Put on warm clothes and some boots. Bring your overnight gear in your backpack."

Before too long, we were riding on horses up a hill and into some trees.

"Where are we going?" I asked.

"We're camping out," said Aunt Suzan.

We rode for an hour. Whenever we came out of the trees, Aunt Suzan made her horse go faster. So my horse went faster, too.

Bounce! Bounce! Bounce!

My bottom felt as if it was being used for a football. I thought the ride would never end.

After a long time, we stopped at the foot of a tall mountain. When I got off the horse, my legs had forgotten how to walk. I wobbled around like a baby taking its first steps.

"I love sleeping under the stars," said Aunt Suzan as she unpacked her backpack.

"You're joking," I said. "We're not sleeping here!" I looked down at the hard ground.

"Yes, we are," said Aunt Suzan, tossing two sleeping bags at me.

By the time I'd rolled the sleeping bags out, Aunt Suzan had poured us a cup of hot soup.

I heard a scratching noise in the tree behind me. "What's that?" I asked.

"Maybe a gorilla," said Aunt Suzan.

"We don't have gorillas!" I said, laughing.

"It must be a possum then," she said.

I finished my soup and looked around.

"Where's the bathroom?" I asked.

"Ahh!" said Aunt Suzan with a laugh. "There are two bathrooms. Yours is behind that tree. Mine is behind that one."

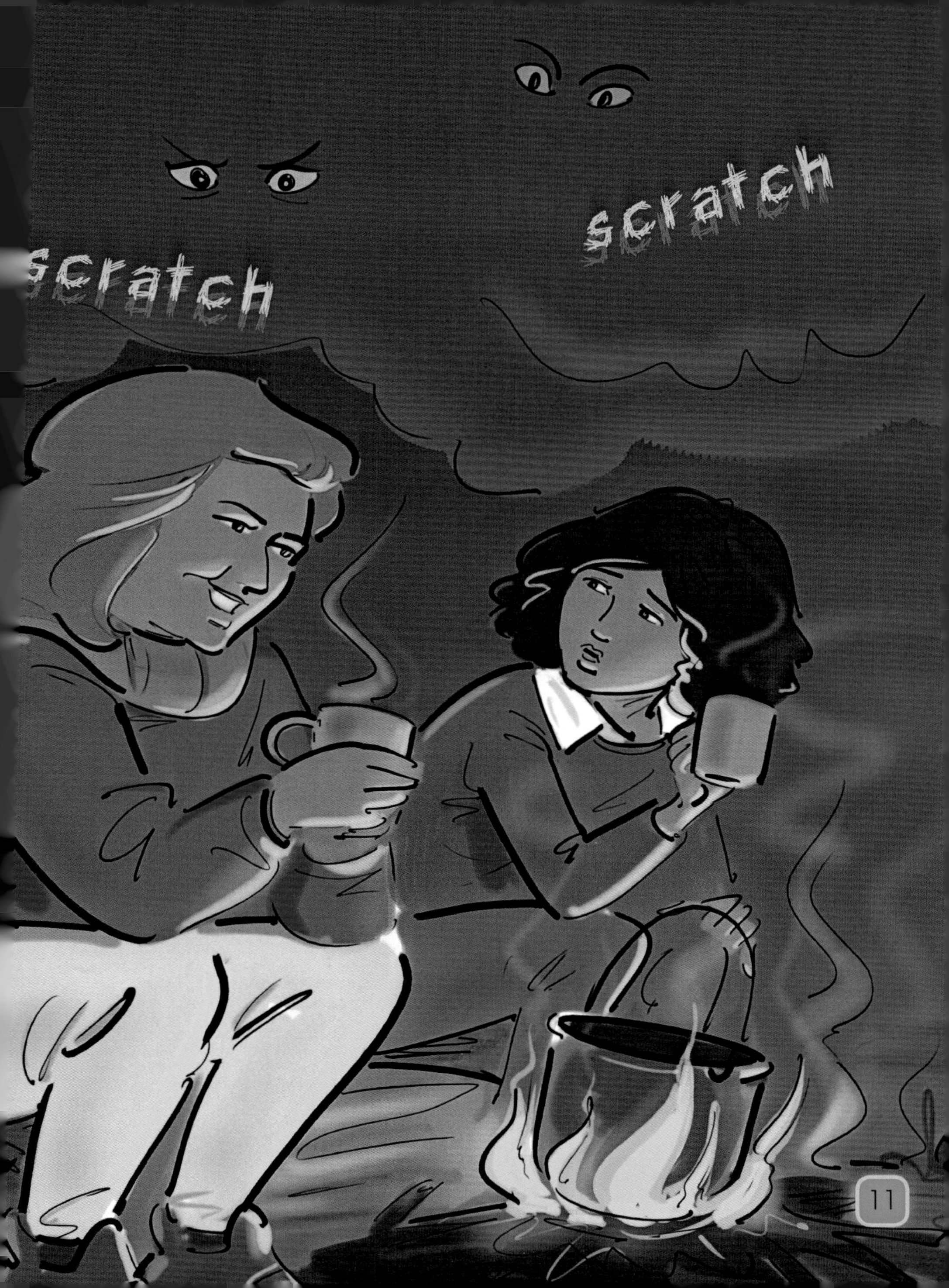
scratch
scratch

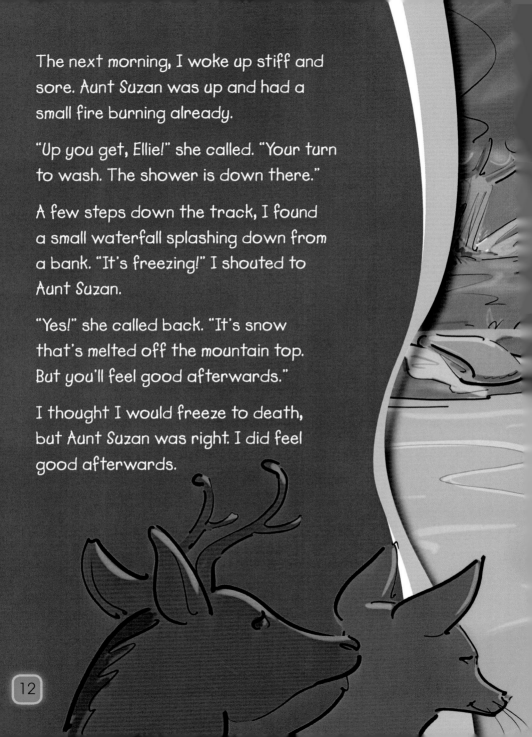

The next morning, I woke up stiff and sore. Aunt Suzan was up and had a small fire burning already.

"Up you get, Ellie!" she called. "Your turn to wash. The shower is down there."

A few steps down the track, I found a small waterfall splashing down from a bank. "It's freezing!" I shouted to Aunt Suzan.

"Yes!" she called back. "It's snow that's melted off the mountain top. But you'll feel good afterwards."

I thought I would freeze to death, but Aunt Suzan was right. I did feel good afterwards.

"What are we doing today?" I asked as I ate my sausages.

"Going up there," said Aunt Suzan, pointing a sausage at the mountain.

"Won't the horses get tired?" I asked.

"No, they won't get tired," said Aunt Suzan. "They're not going."

I looked at the horses. I looked at Aunt Suzan. Then I looked up at the mountain. "You mean we're going to walk all the way?" I asked quietly.

"Yep!" replied Aunt Suzan. "We'll have to hurry, though. It's a five-hour walk to the top and back, and I've booked us in at Fun Park this evening. I'm looking forward to riding on the roller coaster again. And the racing cars. I love the speed and thrills of the racing track."

I couldn't believe it. I'd come to Great-aunt Suzan's thinking I would be bored out of my brain. I thought I'd have to sit around doing nothing. But I was being run off my feet in a non-stop race. Maybe I was wrong about old people.

"Aunt Suzan," I said. "When do you water the pot plants and watch TV?"

"What?" asked Aunt Suzan. "What are you talking about, Ellie?"

"Nothing," I said, laughing. "Let's get going. I'd hate to be late for Fun Park."

You Know What Old People Are Like is a **Recount.**

A **recount** tells . . .

- **who** the story is about (the characters)
- **when** the story happened
- **where** the story is set.

Who	When	Where
	The weekend I went to stay with Great-aunt Suzan	

recount tells what happens.

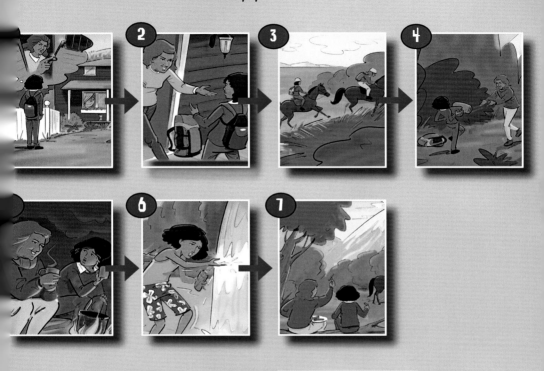

A recount has a **conclusion**.

Guide Notes

Title: You Know What Old People Are Like

Stage: Fluency

Text Form: Recount

Approach: Guided Reading

Processes: Thinking Critically, Exploring Language, Processing Information

Written and Visual Focus: Illustrative Text, Thought Bubbles

THINKING CRITICALLY
(sample questions)
- What do you think this story could be about? Look at the title and discuss.
- Look at the cover. Why do you think the woman is looking out of her window?
- Look at pages 2 and 3. Why do you think Ellie thinks watering pot plants and watching TV is boring?
- Look at pages 4 and 5. How do you think Ellie felt when she met Aunt Suzan at the door?
- Look at pages 6 and 7. Do you think Ellie is an experienced horse rider? Why or why not?
- Look at pages 8 and 9. What do you think Ellie meant when she said *my legs had forgotten how to walk*?
- Look at pages 12 and 13. Why do you think Ellie felt good after her shower?
- Look at pages 14 and 15. How do you think Ellie feels about walking up the mountain? Why do you think that?
- Do you think Ellie will go to stay with Aunt Suzan again? Why or why not?

EXPLORING LANGUAGE

Terminology
Spread, author and illustrator credits, imprint information, ISBN number

Vocabulary
Clarify: stiff, prison, gorilla, possum, melted, great-aunt
Adjectives: *boring* days, *five-hour* walk, *old* people
Pronouns: I, they, you, me, she, we, her
Abbreviation: TV
Simile: I wobbled around *like a baby taking its first steps*
Focus the students' attention on **homonyms**, **antonyms** and **synonyms** if appropriate.

Print Conventions
Apostrophe – possessive (Aunt Suzan's gate)
Hyphens (five-hour, non-stop, Great-aunt)